COMMON CORE CLINICS

Grade 3

English Language Arts

Writing and Language

Common Core Clinics, English Language Arts, Writing and Language, Grade 3
OT222 / 334NA

ISBN-13: 978-0-7836-8663-9

Cover Image: © Photodisc/Thinkstock

Triumph Learning® 136 Madison Avenue, 7th Floor, New York, NY 10016

© 2012 Triumph Learning, LLC
Coach is an imprint of Triumph Learning®

ALL ABOUT YOUR BOOK

COMMON CORE CLINICS will help you master important reading skills.

Each lesson has a **Learn About It** box that teaches the idea. A sample passage focuses on the skill. A **graphic organizer** shows you a reading strategy.

Each lesson has a **Try It** passage with **guided reading**.

 **Higher-Order Thinking Skills**

Questions that make you think further about what you read.

Apply It provides **independent practice** for reading passages, answering short-answer questions, and responding to writing prompts.

Table of Contents

Write an Opinion

Learn About It

An **opinion** is what someone thinks, feels, or believes. When you write something that states your opinion, you need to support it with **facts**, **reasons**, and **details**. At the end of your piece, **summarize** your argument in a **conclusion**.

Read the paragraph. Look for the writer's opinion and the facts, reasons, and details that support the opinion.

The mayor wants to build a new baseball stadium. I do not think that the city should build a stadium. Houses and stores would have to be torn down to make room for it. The stadium would also take the place of parks and playgrounds in the center of the city. Also, traffic would cause problems for the people still in the neighborhood.

Claim	The city should not build a baseball stadium.
Reason	Houses and stores would have to be torn down.
Reason	The stadium would replace parks and playgrounds.
Reason	Traffic would be a problem.
Conclusion	There are many reasons why we should not build a baseball stadium.

Try It

Read the passage. Underline the sentence that states the opinion. Place a star next to each detail that tells you more about the opinion. Use the questions to help you.

Every Day Should Be P.E. Day

Public schools in our state have physical education (P.E.) for students in grade school just two days a week. I believe that we should have P.E. every day of the week. More children than ever are overweight. Being physically active is important for keeping a healthy weight.

> What is the writer's opinion?

According to health experts, children should get sixty minutes of exercise daily. The National Heart Association suggests that children should get at least thirty minutes of exercise during the school day. This would help students get in the habit of regular exercise. This will help them throughout their lives.

Many studies have shown that exercise also helps students concentrate better. That means that teachers would not have to deal as often with students who cause problems in the classroom because they cannot focus. It seems obvious that many students would behave better if they "worked off" some extra energy.

> What reasons does the writer use to support his or her opinion?

I also think that having P.E. on every school day would help students look forward to coming to school. Many children look forward to playing games, jumping rope, dancing, and the other activities that take place in P.E. If students got to go to P.E. every day, they would enjoy school more.

Physical education is an important part of education. There are many reasons that students should have P.E. every day.

HOTS Evaluate

What other reasons could the author add to further support his or her opinion?

Apply It

Read the writing prompt. Plan your response in the graphic organizer.

PROMPT

Many people have pets. Different people think that different animals make the best pet. Choose an animal that you think makes the best pet. Write why you chose this animal and why it makes the best pet.

Opinion	
Reason	
Reason	
Reason	
Conclusion	

Write your response on the lines below.

_____

_____

_____

_____

_____

_____

_____

_____

_____

_____

Write an Informative Piece

Learn About It

> An **informative piece** tells about a topic. When you write something that informs the reader, you need to include **facts**, **definitions**, and **details**, and present your information clearly. Use linking words like *and*, *also*, and *but* to connect ideas. At the end of your piece, include a summary of the information in a **conclusion**.

Read the paragraph. Look at the facts, definitions, and details that tell more about the topic.

One of the best-known zoos in the United States is the San Diego Zoo. It has more than 4,000 animals! Many of them are rare species, or kinds of animals. The zoo works to protect these animals so that the species can continue. The giant pandas are among the most popular. There are many reasons that the San Diego Zoo is one of the most popular in the world.

Topic	San Diego Zoo
Fact	The zoo has over 4,000 animals.
Definiton	**Species** means "kind of animal."
Fact	The zoo helps to protect animals.
Fact	Popular animals include pandas.
Conclusion	There are many reasons why the San Diego Zoo is one of the most popular in the world.

Try It

Read the passage. Underline the sentence that states the topic. Place a star next to each linking word, such as *and* or *but*. Use the questions to help you.

The Largest Mammal That Lived on Land

After the dinosaurs became extinct, mammals still survived. As time went on, some very large mammals came into being. The largest mammal that we know of was the *indricotherium* (pronounced *in dri koh THEER ee uhm*). This cousin of the rhinoceros stood close to 16 feet tall! In fact, it was as big as a house. Like a rhinoceros, the indricotherium had three toes on each foot. Unlike the rhinoceros, it had long legs and a long neck. It also did not have horns.

What is the topic of the passage?

This giant mammal did not eat meat. It was tall enough to eat leaves at the tops of trees. It was so large as an adult that no other animal would try to attack it. However, a baby indricotherium needed its mother to protect it for two to three years.

The indricotherium lived between thirty and sixteen million years ago in Asia. A young scientist first found its fossils in 1932. The fossils were in what is now Pakistan.

What facts, details, and definitions does the author include?

Why did this mammal die out? It seems that forests in Asia got drier and became grasslands. There were not enough plants for this animal to eat. At that point, they became extinct.

Some scientists believe that the indricotherium were nearly as large as the sauropod dinosaurs. They were truly among the world's largest animals ever.

HOTS Evaluate

What else would you like to know about the indricotherium?

Apply It

Read the writing prompt. Plan your response in the graphic organizer.

PROMPT

Choose a place that you would like to visit. Find out facts and details about the place. For example, you might look up how old the place is, details about its history, or things to do and see there. Then write to tell others what you have learned about this place.

Topic	
Fact	
Fact	
Fact	
Conclusion	

Write your response on the lines below.

Write a Narrative

Learn About It

A **narrative** tells a story. When you write a story, it must have a beginning, a middle, and an ending. It must also have **characters**, a **setting**, a **plot**, and a **problem** to solve.

Read the paragraph from a story. Look at the character in the story. What problem is he facing?

Elijah, a nine-year-old boy in Ms. Bremer's class, knows a lot about maps. When it's time for a geography quiz, Elijah feels sure of himself. "I got this," he thinks to himself. But when he gets his paper, his eyes open wide. "Oh, no!" he says to his friend Vanessa. "I know countries, but I don't know states!"

Characters	Elijah, Ms. Bremer, Vanessa
Setting	Ms. Bremer's classroom
Plot	Elijah is taking a geography quiz.
Problem	Elijah does not know the material on the quiz.

Try It

Read the narrative. Underline the name of the characters. Pay attention to the plot. Use the questions to help you.

The Emergency Room Visit

One morning, the Allen family went to visit Grandma. Papa, Mama, and Leonora all were there. Leonora was usually a very happy toddler. She could only say a few words, but she knew how to walk and run. This morning, though, Leonora didn't seem herself. When Grandma tried to hug her, she squirmed away. Mama said to Grandma, "Look how she can walk!" Leonora tried to run away but began to cry.

> Who is the main character?

For the next ninety minutes, Leonora cried. Grandma made funny faces at Leonora. Leonora cried. Mama got a snack for Leonora. Leonora cried. Papa tried to chase Leonora. Leonora cried. When she walked, she had a limp. Then she cried some more.

> Where does the first part of the story take place?

"Oh, no, I think something's really wrong!" said Papa.

"Me, too," said Mama. "It looks like there's a problem with her foot. The doctor's office is closed, though. We'll have to bring her to the emergency room." The family left Grandma's house and headed off to the hospital.

At the emergency room, a nurse asked Mama, "What's the problem?"

> What happens in the beginning, middle, and end of the story?

"My baby is limping. She seems like she's in terrible pain when she walks. And she won't stop crying!" said Mama.

The nurse gave Mama forms to fill out. Soon a doctor came to take an X-ray of Leonora's foot. When the doctor took off Leonora's shoe to examine her foot, the little girl stopped crying. The doctor showed Papa and Mama Leonora's red toe. Her problem was that she'd outgrown her shoe!

HOTS Analyze

What might happen when the Allen family leaves the hospital?

Apply It

Read the writing prompt. Plan your response in the graphic organizer.

PROMPT

Write about a child your age who is having a problem. Use ideas from your own life or make up the story completely. Be sure to have one event lead to the next, and have a beginning, middle, and end. Clearly state where and when the story takes place.

Characters	
Setting	
Plot	
Problem	

Write your response on the lines below.

_____

_____

_____

_____

_____

_____

_____

_____

_____

_____

_____

Nouns

Learn About It

A **noun** is a word that names a person, animal, place, thing, or idea. A noun can name a thing that you can touch, like *pencil*. An **abstract noun** names a thing that you cannot touch, like *happiness*. When a noun names just one person, animal, place, or thing, it is **singular**. If a noun names more than one person, animal, place, or thing, it is **plural**. Nouns can be **regular** or **irregular**.

Read the paragraph. Look for the nouns.

My father keeps a book of photographs. They show a trip he took to Mexico many years ago. He went to see his grandmothers. He always feels happiness when he looks at the book. He and his cousins were just children then. In the photographs, some are still missing baby teeth. Today, they all share great memories of that time.

Types of Nouns	Singular	Plural
Regular Nouns	Book	Books
	Father	Fathers
	Tax	Taxes
Irregular Nouns	Child	Children
	Mouse	Mice
	Tooth	Teeth

Nouns You Can Touch	Abstract Nouns
Dinner	Memory
Grandmother	Age
Photograph	Happiness

Try It

Read the passage. Underline the nouns. Circle the irregular plural nouns. Draw a box around any abstract nouns. Use the questions to help you.

Museum Day

(1) Eva and Joan went with their class to three museums on Saturday. (2) They had a great time. (3) In the first museum, they saw beautiful paintings. (4) Artists painted the pictures many years ago. (5) Eva and Joan wished that they could paint so well.

> Remember that words like *memory, love,* and *happiness* are abstract nouns. Is *time* an abstract noun in sentence 2?

(6) Then Eva and Joan went with the other children to the science museum. (7) There they looked at different kinds of fish. (8) A scientist showed them different small mammals. (9) They saw gerbils, rats, and mice! (10) Afterward, they got pencils and paper. (11) They got to draw their favorite animals from memory. (12) On some of the pictures, it was hard to tell what was a rat and what was a mouse.

(13) After the science museum, Eva and Joan went with their classmates to the Discovery Museum. (14) This has many different kinds of exhibits. (15) They learned about science here, too. (16) They also learned about social studies. (17) The museum has a town for children to explore. (18) There is a bank, an airport, a market, and a town hall. (19) They got to elect a class government, just for the day!

> Words like *teeth, oxen,* and *deer* are irregular plural nouns. Where is the first irregular plural noun in the passage?

 **HOTS Understand**

Why is it necessary to know which nouns are irregular?

Apply It

Read the passage. Answer the questions on the next page.

Meet the Author

(1) One day, an author came to visit our school. (2) Her name is Pam Flowers. (3) She writes about her own adventures. (4) She has traveled throughout the Arctic with her sled dogs. (5) On the trip, she and the dogs braved terrible storms. (6) They saw moose, eagles, and caribou. (7) Together they learned about trust. (8) The dogs had to trust their leader. (9) The author had to trust the dogs, even though some of them were not always well-behaved.

(10) During the middle of one trip, the dogs refused to pull her sled. (11) They would not go any farther, no matter what Pam Flowers did. (12) They all had to take a day off together. (13) In the end, the author was glad they got a rest.

(14) Pam Flowers showed us slides of her trips. (15) She got the idea of traveling across the Arctic from a book she had read. (16) Making the trip was a dream come true for her. (17) Since then, she has walked the entire Appalachian Trail, which goes from Maine to Georgia. (18) She and her dog Ellie walked over 2,000 miles! (19) They saw all kinds of wildlife, including deer, bears, and squirrels.

(20) Pam Flowers encouraged us to follow our dreams. (21) I wish I could go on adventures like hers! (22) I loved hearing about her journeys. (23) We even got to meet her dog Ellie! (24) That was my favorite part of the visit.

Use "Meet the Author" to answer the questions. Write your answers in complete sentences.

1. What are the three nouns in sentence 1? Choose one of the nouns and write a new sentence using the plural form.

_____

_____

2. What plural nouns in sentence 6 are irregular? Write a new sentence using one of the words.

_____

_____

3. What is the abstract noun in sentence 7? Write a new sentence using the noun.

_____

_____

4. Which noun is abstract in sentence 16? Write a new sentence using the noun.

_____

_____

5. Write a new sentence using the singular form of *deer*.

_____

Learn About It

A **verb** is an action word. Verbs have different **tenses**, which tell when something happens. If an action happens now, use the **present tense**. If an action happened earlier, use the **past tense**. If an action will happen in the future, use the **future tense**. Most past tense verbs end with *-ed*. An irregular verb uses a different form in the past tense.

Read the sentences. Look for the verbs.

My sister and I walk to school in a hurry. Yesterday we walked quickly, but we were still late.

Regular Verb Present	Regular Verb Past
My sister and I **walk**	Yesterday we **walked**

Regular Verb	
Tense	**Example**
Past	Stored
Present	Store, stores
Future	Will store

Irregular Verbs			
Tense		**Examples**	
Past	Gave	Was, were	Grew
Present	Give, gives	Is, are	Grow, grows
Future	Will give	Will be	Will grow

Try It

Read the passage. Underline the regular verbs. Circle the past tense verbs. Draw a box around the irregular verbs. Use the questions to help you.

The Garden

(1) My brother Max wanted a garden. (2) My parents said no at first. (3) My brother read more and more about plants. (4) He learned about vegetables and flowers. (5) He did extra chores. (6) Finally, my mother said okay. (7) She took Max to the plant store. (8) They got lots of seeds. (9) Soon we were ready to go!

(10) Now Max and I dig holes in the ground. (11) I pour water in the holes. (12) My mother and father watch us from the porch. (13) "Leave room between rows of seeds," my father says. (14) My mother wants flowers, too. (15) When she was little, she grew pansies every year in a window box.

(16) "Can we grow pansies?" my brother asks her.

(17) "I don't know if they'll grow here, but you can try," she says.

(18) "Can we grow tulips?" I ask.

(19) "They grow from bulbs. (20) You plant those in the fall," my mother says.

(21) "We want plants we can eat! (22) Grow me lettuce and tomatoes!" says my father. (23) We all laugh together.

(24) My brother had a great idea. (25) Growing a garden is great fun!

> Is the word *wanted* regular past tense or irregular past tense in sentence 1?

> Is *said* a regular past tense verb?

Understand

Why is it necessary to know which verbs are irregular?

Apply It

Read the passage. Answer the questions on the next page.

The Three Sisters

(1) The Iroquois have a legend about corn, beans, and squash. (2) According to the legend, these plants are three sisters. (3) They must grow together to do well. (4) Indeed, throughout parts of what is now Central and North America, Native Americans grew these plants together. (5) The bean vines grew up on the corn plants. (6) These vines made the tall stalks of corn stronger. (7) The squash vines grew on the ground near the corn and beans. (8) These vines blocked sunlight, so weeds would not grow. (9) Sometimes Native Americans placed fish in the soil to make it rich.

(10) All three plants still can work together to make the soil good for growing. (11) They work together to make people healthy, too. (12) Corn gives people energy. (13) Beans are full of protein, which makes us strong. (14) Squash has vitamins and minerals. (15) Its seeds are good for oil. (16) The three sisters keep well, too. (17) Squash can be stored for close to a year. (18) Corn can be ground to make corn flour. (19) You can also cook and eat it right away. (20) Beans can be taken from pods, dried, and stored for a very long time. (21) The three sisters are a helpful family!

Use "The Three Sisters" to answer the questions. Write your answers in complete sentences.

1. What is the verb in sentence 1? Is it past or present tense? Write a new sentence using the verb.

_____

_____

2. What is the verb in sentence 7? Is the verb regular or irregular? Write a new sentence using the future tense of the verb.

_____

_____

3. What is the verb in sentence 12? Write a new sentence using the past tense of the verb.

_____

_____

4. What is the verb in sentence 21? What is its past tense?

_____

_____

Subject-Verb Agreement

Learn About It

A **subject** is a person, animal, place, thing, or idea in a sentence that does something. A **verb** is an action word. **Subject-verb agreement** is the match between the form of a noun and the form of a verb.

Read the paragraph. Look for subject-verb agreement.

A hurricane spins wild winds. Hurricanes form over oceans. They can be frightening. Sometimes they bring terrible storms on land. Hurricanes might bring a tornado, too. A hurricane often causes flooding. People should try to stay out of the way of a hurricane.

Subject	Verb	Correct Verb Ending
Hurricane (singular)	Spins	-s
Hurricanes (plural)	Form	(no additional ending)
They (plural)	Can be	(no additional ending)
Hurricanes (plural)	Bring	(no additional ending)
Hurricane (singular)	Causes	-s
People (plural)	Try	(no additional ending)

Try It

Read the passage. Underline the subjects. Circle the verbs. Put a star next to any sentences where the verb does not agree with the subject. Use the questions to help you.

Ants

(1) Ants is such interesting insects! (2) They are constantly busy, and they are extremely hard workers. (3) Ants lives in groups called colonies. (4) Some large colonies contain millions of ants.

> Does the verb in sentence 1 agree with the noun?

(5) Four different types of ants live in a colony. (6) Each type have a different job. (7) The queen ant lays the egg. (8) She are larger than the other ants. (9) Typically, there is only one queen ant in a colony. (10) A colony have only a few male ants. (11) Male ants and the queen ant create baby ants. (12) Worker ants builds the nest and searches for food. (13) They also take care of the baby ants. (14) Soldier ants protect the other members of the colony. (15) Both worker ants and soldier ants are females.

> Does the verb in sentence 6 agree with the subject? Why or why not?

(16) Ants are found practically everywhere on Earth. (17) So is the stories about them! (18) They are often used as story characters in many cultures of the world.

HOTS Evaluate

How do subject-verb agreement errors affect your understanding of a sentence?

Apply It

Read the passage. It contains mistakes. Answer the questions on the next page.

A Good Vacation

(1) The Jackson family begins planning their summer vacation in March. (2) First, Mrs. Jackson go on the Internet to look at various possibilities. (3) At the same time, Mr. Jackson goes to the library to look at travel books. (4) Then they speaks to their children, Richard and Paula, about where they might like to go. (5) The children's opinions is important to them. (6) Finally, they reach a decision. (7) They will go visit some famous parks in the western United States.

(8) During the next few weeks, the Jacksons research transportation for the trip. (9) They need to decide whether to take a car, a bus, or a plane. (10) They decide a flight is best for them. (11) They look at hotels and airline flights that meet their family's needs. (12) They also wants to be sure they gets the best price.

(13) Meanwhile, Paula and Richard read many travel books. (14) They want to learn about the places they will visit. (15) By April, the Jacksons have arranged to tour the Grand Canyon in Arizona and Bryce Canyon in Utah. (16) Working as a team, they gather all the maps, books, and brochures they need. (17) They also plan what clothes, shoes, and bags they will bring. (18) Now they can hardly wait for the trip!

Use "A Good Vacation" to answer the questions. Write your answers in complete sentences.

1. Rewrite sentence 2 to make the subject and verb agree.

_____

_____

2. Is the correct form of the verb used so that it agrees with the subject in sentence 4? Explain.

_____

_____

3. Rewrite sentence 5 so that the verb agrees with the subject.

_____

_____

4. Does the verb in sentence 9 agree with the subject? Explain.

_____

_____

5. Rewrite sentence 12 so that the verbs match the subjects.

_____

_____

Pronoun-Antecedent Agreement

Learn About It

A **pronoun** takes the place of a noun. There are **subject pronouns**, such as *I, you, he,* and *she*. There are **object pronouns**, such as *me, you, him,* and *her*. There are **possessive pronouns**, such as *mine, yours, his,* and *hers*. A pronoun has to agree with the noun it is replacing, which is called the **antecedent**. A pronoun must match its antecedent in number, person, and gender.

Read the paragraph. Look for the pronouns and the nouns they replace.

Ben and Denise take an art class. They love it! Ben drew lots of pictures last week. He wants to work more on them this week. Denise finished a painting last week. She was pretty happy with it.

Antecedent	Pronoun That Replaces the Noun
Ben and Denise	They
Art class	It
Ben	He
Pictures	Them
Denise	She
Painting	It

Subject Pronouns	Object Pronouns	Possessive Pronouns
I	Me	Mine
You	You	Yours
He	Him	His
She	Her	Hers
It	It	Its
We	Us	Ours
They	Them	Theirs

Try It

Read the passage. Underline the subject pronouns. Circle the object pronouns. Use the questions to help you.

A Saturday Movie

(1) Michael was sleeping peacefully on Saturday when his younger sister, Matilda, dashed into his room. (2) "It's time to wake up, Michael!" she shouted at him. (3) "Don't you remember that we are supposed to go to the movies today?" (4) Michael remembered, of course, and he quickly scrambled out of bed, got dressed, and ate some breakfast. (5) Then he and Matilda walked the four long city blocks to the movie theater. (6) As they approached the theater, there was a line forming. (7) "Aren't you glad we got here early?" said Matilda.

(8) "I am," said Michael.

(9) "Do you think we should get some popcorn?" he asked his sister.

(10) "That line is long, too," said Matilda.

(11) "Oh, wait—there's my friend Janie inside. We can ask her to get it for us," said Michael.

(12) They called to Janie. (13) She agreed to take their money and buy some popcorn. (14) When the movie started, all three friends were in their seats to enjoy it.

> What noun in sentence 2 does the pronoun *she* refer to?

> What does *it* in sentence 14 refer to?

Analyze

Why are pronouns an important part of speech?

Apply It

Read the passage. It contains mistakes. Answer the questions on the next page.

Earning It

(1) Steven examined his brand new, red bicycle and smiled. (2) He had worked very hard for seven months to get this bike, and now they was his! (3) He thought back to November when he had first asked Mom and Dad for a new bicycle. (4) He had seen the perfect model at a bicycle shop in town. (5) Mom and Dad explained that he would have to help out and earn some of the money himself. (6) At first, Steven was disappointed that they didn't just buy him the bike. (7) He knew that his friend Raul's parents had bought him a bike, and so Steven told his parents. (8) "We are not Raul's parents," his mother said. (9) So Steven went to work.

(10) In the past seven months, Steven had done a variety of jobs to earn money. (11) He ran errands for neighbors, shoveled mountains of snow, and walked the neighborhood dogs. (12) Doing all that work, she had saved quite a tidy sum. (13) Then his parents added the rest of the money that he needed to buy the bicycle he had picked out.

(14) This morning, he bought your new bike. (15) "We are very proud of you," his parents told him. (16) As a matter of fact, Steven was very proud of himself!

Use "Earning It" to answer the questions. Write your answers in complete sentences.

1. What does the pronoun *he* refer to in sentence 2?

   _____

   _____

2. What is the pronoun-antecedent mistake in sentence 2?

   _____

   _____

3. Who does the pronoun *they* refer to in sentence 6?

   _____

   _____

4. What is the mistake in sentence 12? Rewrite the sentence correctly.

   _____

   _____

5. What is the mistake in sentence 14? Rewrite the sentence correctly.

   _____

   _____

Adjectives

Learn About It

An **adjective** is a word that describes a noun or pronoun. If you are comparing two things, you use a **comparative adjective**. If you are comparing more than two things, you use a **superlative adjective**.

Read the passage. Look for the adjectives.

On the most beautiful day of spring, the three goats tried to cross the bridge. The smallest goat went first. As he crossed, he heard a terrible voice, saying, "Who dares to cross my bridge?"

"It is I," the small goat said. "Do not eat me, for I have a bigger brother who will be crossing soon. He will make a nicer meal than I."

The bad troll under the bridge let the first goat cross.

Types of Adjectives	To Describe One	To Compare Two	To Compare More than Two
Regular	Small	Smaller	Smallest
	Nice	Nicer	Nicest
	Big	Bigger	Biggest
Irregular	Good	Better	Best
	Bad	Worse	Worst
Three Syllables or More	Beautiful	More beautiful	Most beautiful
	Terrible	More terrible	Most terrible

Try It

Read the passage. Underline the adjectives. Circle the comparative adjectives. Draw a box around the superlative adjectives. Use the questions to help you.

Trying at Tennis

(1) Donovan was determined to be the best tennis player at camp. (2) There were other boys who were bigger and faster than him. (3) Some girls were very good players, too. (4) But Donovan tried the hardest. (5) When he came home from camp, after playing for five hours already, he would hit the ball against the garage wall. (6) He got so good that he almost never missed the ball.

> **What is the superlative adjective in sentence 1?**

(7) Donovan's coach knew that in some ways, Donovan was a worse player than others. (8) He had a harder time serving the ball because he did not have as much experience. (9) Therefore, the coach did not want to put Donovan on his junior tennis team at the end of the summer. (10) Donovan was crushed. (11) He asked the coach if he could have another chance to prove himself. (12) The coach said all right, so Donovan went to camp early every day with a bucket of balls. (13) He practiced serving again and again, tossing the ball high into the air and reaching with his racket to hit the ball. (14) After about a week, the coach saw how much Donovan's game had improved.

> **What is the comparative adjective in sentence 8?**

(15) "Why, by next year," Coach said, "you really might be our best player."

HOTS Understand

How can you tell the difference between a comparative adjective and a superlative adjective?

Apply It

Read the passage. It contains mistakes. Answer the questions on the next page.

The Three Little Goldfish

(1) Once there were three little goldfish. (2) The oldest was the biggest and most adventurous. (3) The youngest was the smallest and shyest. (4) The middle fish was the faster. (5) One day, the oldest fish said, "Let's go see the world!" (6) The youngest fish was scared, and tried to hide behind a colorful coral reef. (7) The middle fish was fast enough to catch the youngest, and so off the three fish went.

(8) "Maybe we'll find a treasure chest," said the oldest fish. (9) The middle fish, who was wiser than the oldest, said, "Maybe we can join a school and learn about the world!" (10) The smallest fish just wanted to get home safely.

(11) On the first day of their journey, the fish were full of energy. (12) On the second day, they were a little more tired. (13) On the third day, the fish decided to rest and feast on some delicious algae. (14) But as they slowed down, the most littlest yelled, "Shark!" (15) The three goldfish swam behind a rock and watched the shark pass by. (16) The biggest fish glanced down. (17) "A treasure chest," it cried. (18) The fish opened it and each swam away with a strand of gold. (19) "A school!" the middle fish cried, and darted toward it. (20) The three fish joined the school and learned about the ocean. (21) After a few days, they headed back home and got there safely. (22) Each fish got its wish.

Use "The Three Little Goldfish" to answer the questions. Write your answers in complete sentences.

1. What are the adjectives in sentence 2? Are they comparative or superlative?

_____

_____

2. Rewrite sentence 4 correctly.

_____

_____

3. What is the superlative form of *wiser*? Write a new sentence using the superlative form.

_____

_____

4. What adjective describes fish food in sentence 13?

_____

_____

5. Rewrite sentence 14 correctly.

_____

_____

Adverbs

Learn About It

An **adverb** tells about a verb, an adjective, or another adverb. Adverbs can tell about how, where, or when an action or actions happen. Many adverbs end in *-ly*. Some adverbs compare one action to another. These are **comparative adverbs**. Some adverbs compare one action to two or more other actions. These are **superlative adverbs**.

Read the paragraph. Look for adverbs.

My father cooks faster than my mother cooks. He can make a tasty stir fry dinner sooner than I can set the table. He complains loudly that we don't appreciate his cooking, but it's not true. More frequently than not, I enjoy his ten-minute meals.

Types of Adverb	To Describe One Action	To Compare Two Actions	To Compare More than Two Actions
Adverbs That Tell *How*	Fast	Faster	Fastest
	Loudly	More loudly	Most loudly
	Surprisingly	More surprisingly	Most surprisingly
Adverbs That Tell *Where*	Near	Nearer	Nearest
	Far	Farther	Farthest
Adverbs That Tell *When*	Soon	Sooner	Soonest
	Frequently	More frequently	Most frequently

Try It

Read the passage. Underline the adverbs. Circle the words the adverbs describe. Use the questions to help you.

Don't Get Lost

(1) Eva carefully wrote directions to her party. (2) She explained that the bowling alley where they were meeting was in a nearby town. (3) She included how to get there by bus or by car.

(4) When she handed out the invitations, she pointed out the directions and told her friends, "Now don't get lost."

> **What word does the adverb *carefully* describe in sentence 1?**

(5) "Why don't you have your party at the bowling alley that's closer to your house?" asked Andre.

(6) "Why don't you ask my parents?" Eva said jokingly.

(7) "Um, that's okay," Andre said quietly.

(8) On the day of the party, a group of friends met at the bus stop and got on the first bus that came. (9) "Wait a minute," said Andre worriedly. (10) "I don't see the names of the streets that Eva wrote. (11) I think this bus is taking us farther from the party!"

> **What word in sentence 6 describes how Eva said something?**

(12) "Where do you need to go?" asked the bus driver kindly.

(13) Andre told him the name of the bowling alley, and the bus driver shook his head. (14) "You're okay," he explained. (15) "The street you're looking for is coming up. (16) The bowling alley is not too far from here. (17) Next time, though, check carefully before you get on the bus!"

HOTS Understand

In what way would sentence 12 be different if you removed the adverb?

Apply It

Read the passage. It contains mistakes. Answer the questions on the next page.

Philemon and Baucis

(1) Long ago there was a town where people treated strangers cruelly. (2) On a hill outside the town lived an old man, Philemon, and an old woman, Baucis, who treated everyone kindly. (3) One day, two strangers came through town and were treated poorly. (4) When Philemon and Baucis saw the strangers coming, they welcomed them warmly and invited them to dinner.

(5) As the strangers entered, Baucis apologized for having so little food and drink. (6) Yet the strangers asked for glass after glass of milk. (7) To Baucis's surprise, milk kept flowing from the pitcher! (8) The short stranger spoke merrilier than the tall stranger. (9) Philemon and Baucis invited the two to spend the night, and the strangers happily accepted.

(10) In the morning, the old couple was shocked to find a lake where the town had so recently stood. (11) The two strangers admitted that they were Zeus and Hermes, and that they had punished the townspeople by turning them into fish. (12) Baucis and Philemon were even more surprised to find their hut turned into a marble palace.

(13) "You have treated us more kindly than your neighbors did," Zeus explained. (14) "Let us grant you any wish you have."

(15) The old people explained quietly that they wished to live and die together. (16) Zeus and Hermes quickly agreed to this wish. (17) After living to a very old age, Baucis and Philemon died at the same moment. (18) They changed into a pair of beautiful trees that grew together.

Use "Philemon and Baucis" to answer the questions. Write your answers in complete sentences.

1. What is the adverb that describes how townspeople treated others in sentence 1?

_____

_____

2. What word explains how Philemon and Baucis behave toward others?

_____

_____

3. Rewrite sentence 8 using the correct form of the comparative adverb.

_____

_____

4. What is the superlative form of the adverb in sentence 13? Write a new sentence using the superlative form.

_____

_____

Types of Sentences

Learn About It

There are different kinds of sentences. A **simple sentence** contains only one subject and verb, and tells a complete thought. A simple sentence is also called an **independent clause**. A **compound sentence** has two independent clauses joined by a word like *and*, *but*, or *or*. A **complex sentence** includes one independent clause and one dependent clause. A **dependent clause** has a subject and a verb but cannot stand alone as a sentence. Dependent clauses often start with words like *after*, *although*, or *if*.

Read the paragraph. Look for simple, compound, and complex sentences.

The stegosaurus was one surprising animal! While the stegosaurus was 30 feet long, its brain was only the size of a golf ball. This dinosaur ate plants, and it lived in the Midwest of the United States.

Sentence Type	What It Contains	Example
Simple	Subject + verb	The stegosaurus was one surprising animal!
Compound	Independent clause + independent clause	This dinosaur ate plants, and it lived in the Midwest of the United States.
Complex	Dependent clause + independent clause	While the stegosaurus was 30 feet long, its brain was only the size of a golf ball.

Try It

Read the passage. Underline simple sentences. Put a star next to compound sentences. Circle dependent clauses in complex sentences. Use the questions to help you.

Seismographs and Earthquakes

(1) Seismographs, or machines that figure out the size of an earthquake, have been around since 1880. (2) Geologists use seismographs to study earthquakes. (3) These devices measure Earth's movements, and they tell how fast the movements are happening. (4) They also record the movements.

> Is sentence 2 simple or compound? How many subjects and verbs do you see?

(5) Scientists have long tried to identify the size of earthquakes. (6) To do so, they have looked at damage to buildings, people, and nature. (7) In the late 19th century, European scientists introduced a ten-point scale to describe earthquakes. (8) The most damaging earthquakes have the highest numbers. (9) In the United States today, scientists use a twelve-point scale. (10) If Earth's movement falls below 3 on the scale, most people would barely feel a tremor. (11) If Earth's movement falls above 7 on the scale, disaster may be underway.

> Is sentence 3 compound or complex? How many independent clauses do you see?

(12) Along with measuring earthquakes, scientists have also studied why they happen. (13) Earth's surface is made up of a series of thick plates. (14) Where the plates are separated, faults exist. (15) Earthquakes often occur along the fault lines. (16) Far under the earth, huge pieces of rock move. (17) When the pieces collide and release energy, we get earthquakes.

> Sentence 17 is a complex sentence. What is the dependent clause?

(18) When earthquakes occur, seismic waves travel near or through the earth. (19) The seismograph actually measures these waves. (20) A tsunami is a huge ocean wave. (21) A tsunami sometimes results from earthquakes on the floor of the ocean.

HOTS Understand

Why is it important to write using different kinds of sentences?

Apply It

Read the passage. Answer the questions on the next page.

Earth Day

(1) What are you doing on April 22nd? (2) Maybe you can take part in an Earth Day event. (3) More than forty years ago, Americans came together to try to help Earth. (4) They organized the first official Earth Day, on April 22, 1970. (5) On that day, volunteers around the country tried to teach others about pollution. (6) They gave out information about ways that everyone can help take care of the planet.

(7) The founder of Earth Day was a man named Gaylord Nelson, who was a senator from Wisconsin. (8) After seeing how oil spills in California destroyed wildlife, Nelson was determined to take action. (9) He got support from Democrats and Republicans for his cause. (10) A graduate student named Denis Hayes dropped out of Harvard, and he organized events across the United States. (11) In the end, over 20 million people protested air and water pollution on that first Earth Day.

(12) Did Earth Day lead to any changes? (13) In fact, it had several important results. (14) The United States government formed the Environmental Protection Agency. (15) Lawmakers passed laws that made industries find ways to reduce pollution, and they passed the Endangered Species Act. (16) This helped protect species of animals that are at risk of completely dying out.

(17) Earth Day continues every year. (18) If you check your local newspaper or community Web site, you will probably find an event near you!

Use "Earth Day" to answer the questions. Write your answers in complete sentences.

1. What kind of sentence is sentence 6?

_____

_____

2. Why is sentence 7 a complex sentence?

_____

_____

3. How could you expand sentence 9 and rewrite it as a compound sentence?

_____

_____

4. How would you rewrite sentence 10 as two simple sentences?

_____

_____

5. How could you rewrite sentence 18 as a compound sentence?

_____

_____

Capitals and Punctuation

Learn About It

Capital letters should be used at the beginning of the first word in a sentence. They should also begin names of people, places, and some things. The marks you use when writing sentences are called **punctuation**.

Read the paragraph. Look at what words are capitalized, and look at the different types of punctuation.

Happy birthday to America! Our country announced that it was independent from England on July 4, 1776. How do you celebrate our country's birthday?

When to Use Capitals	Example
At the beginning of sentences	This is a good show.
For people	My favorite character is Carol.
For places	The show is set in Philadelphia.
For important words in titles	The name of the show is <u>Free in Philadelphia.</u>

Punctuation	When to Use It	Example
Comma	In addresses	New York, New York
Comma	At the end of a phrase before the last quotation mark	"I feel good," said Sam.
Comma	In a letter's greeting and closing	Dear Aunt Linda, Love, Sue
Quotation marks	At the beginning and end of dialogue	"I am tired," Carl said.
Apostrophe	To make a word possessive	Country's birthday

Try It

Read the passage and look for mistakes in punctuation and capitalization. Underline the letters that should be capitalized. Circle where quotation marks should appear. Insert any missing commas. Use the questions to help you.

Mark Twain

(1) Mark twain is one of america's most famous writers. (2) Twain wrote *Tom Sawyer* and *The adventures of Huckleberry Finn.* (3) His real name was samuel Clemens, and he was born in Florida Missouri, on November 30, 1835. (4) He set some of his best-known fiction in missouri.

> Are there any other words in sentence 1 that need to be capitalized?

(5) When he was a young man, clemens took a job as a captain on a mississippi steamboat. (6) He also worked as a printer. (7) Before he achieved fame as a writer, Clemens traveled to nevada to be a miner. (8) That didn't work out, so he began to write for the newspaper there instead. (9) If there wasn't enough interesting news, he would sometimes make up stories. (10) During his time as a journalist, Clemens wrote a short story called "The Celebrated Jumping Frog of Calaveras county." (11) This story became extremely popular, and his life as a writer began.

> Where should a comma be placed in sentence 3?

(12) Mark Twain, as he was now known, wrote books about his travels, along with stories and novels. (13) He also was an extremely popular public speaker, and toured the country. (14) "The man with a new idea is called a crank until the idea succeeds, Twain wrote. (15) Twain's new ideas for the novel keep his works alive today.

HOTS Understand

Why is it important to use appropriate capitalization and punctuation?

Apply It

Read the passage. It contains mistakes. Then answer the questions on the next page.

A Letter from California

May 6, 2013

Dear Grandma,

(1) Daddy and I have seen lots of california. (2) My favorite part was driving on the scenic highway. (3) The views were amazing!

(4) Daddy brought a book called *The family Guide to california*, which I read in the car. (5) we tried to figure out the best places to go. (6) We have seen a bunch of state parks and museums, but we could always do more. (7) When we drove up north, Daddy even thought about going farther north, to Seattle Washington. (8) I wanted to head south, so I talked him out of it.

(9) We went to see my cousins John and Sylvia. (10) They said What are you doing here?" (11) I guess we didn't give them enough notice that we were coming. (12) They were still nice to us, though. (13) They told us the best places to hike around Monterey Bay. (14) The Monterey Bay Aquarium is great, too!

(15) I was excited to see Hollywood in Los Angeles, but we didn't spot any stars. (16) Well, we did spot stars on the sidewalk in front of Grauman's Chinese Theatre. (17) Do you know about those? (18) The most famous people in movies put their footprints in wet cement in front of the theater. (19) It's called a walk of stars. (20) I spotted a bunch of my favorites, but there were a lot of people whose names I didn't know. (21) Maybe you've heard of them. (22) When we get back, let's watch some old movies together. (23) Then maybe I'll know whose footprints I saw!

Love,
Louisa

Use "A Letter from California" to answer the questions. Write your answers in complete sentences.

1. What word in sentence 1 needs to be capitalized? Rewrite the sentence correctly.

_____

_____

2. How would you correct sentence 4?

_____

_____

3. What word in sentence 5 needs to be capitalized? Rewrite the sentence correctly.

_____

_____

4. Where should you add a comma in sentence 7? Rewrite sentence 7 correctly.

_____

_____

5. Rewrite sentence 10 correctly.

_____

_____

Spelling

Learn About It

Spelling is the order in which letters form a word. In English, many words follow the same spelling patterns and rules. A **word family** is a group of words that share the same spelling pattern.

Read the paragraph. Use the dictionary to find how to spell the underlined words.

How often do you brush your teeth? Brush them after <u>evry</u> meal and before you go to <u>slep</u> at night. Take your time, and don't brush <u>qickly</u>.

Spelling Rule	Examples
Double consonants in many two-syllable words.	Bubble, middle
To form the past tense, add **-ed**. If the word ends in **e**, just add **-d**.	Planted, lined
To form the past tense to a word ending in **y**, change the **y** to an **i**, and add **-ed**.	Buried, married
To form the plural of a word, add **-s** or **-es**. If the word ends in **y**, change the **y** to an **i**, and add **-es**.	Papers, latches, berries

Word Family	Examples
Ack	Back, crack, jack, pack, quack, rack, sack, tack, whack
Ause	Applause, because, cause, pause
Eigh	Eight, sleigh, weigh, weight
Uit	Fruit, suit

Try It

Read the passage. Underline words that are misspelled. Use the questions to help you.

No More Junk!

(1) Helth experts believe that people are eating too much junk food today. (2) They also think that it's importint for people to develop healthy eating habits at a young age. (3) What foods should we include in our diet? (4) We should eat froots, vegetables, and whole grains, such as whole-wheat bread and brown rice. (5) We should also eat foods with calcium, such as milk, yogurt, and cheese. (6) What foods should we avoid? (7) We shouldn't eat junk food, such as potato chips and candy bars. (8) Junk food contians too much fat and sugar.

> **What word is misspelled in sentence 4?**

(9) Many health experts believe that we would be eating beter if we cookd the food ourselves. (10) When you cook your own food, you know just how much of each ingredient you are using. (11) You can control how much salt you are shaking in the dish. (12) A litle salt is good for us. (13) A lot of salt is very bad. (14) When you cook, though, you have to skip the TV diners. (15) They are fuul of fat and salt. (16) Make yourself a salad or cook on the grill. (17) You will feel beter before you know it!

> **Is more than one word misspelled in sentence 9?**

Apply

What should you do if you are not sure about a word's spelling?

Apply It

Read the passage. It contains mistakes. Answer the questions on the next page.

Check Your Backpack

(1) Recent studys have found that American kids are carrying backpacks that are too heavy. (2) Kids should cary fewir things so they lighten their backpack load. (3) Why? (4) A heavy backpack can cause back and shoulder pain. (5) Over time this can lead to serious back and shoulder problems. (6) Another finding was that uneven backpack loads can cause pain in the lower back.

(7) As children get older, thay can cary heavier bags, but elementry students really should be careful. (8) Experts say that a nine-year-old's backpack should not weigh more than eight pounds. (9) In fact, backpacks should never weigh more than ten percent of a person's weight. (10) One study found that some nine-year-olds were actually carrying more than twelve pounds in their backpacks. (11) That is much too heavy!

(12) Another problem is that many students carry there backpacks over just one shoulder. (13) That means there's too much weight on one side, which can cause neck and back pain. (14) Doctors have some suggestions. (15) One is that shoulder straps on backpacks should be wide and well-padded. (16) They should also be adjusted for a snug fit. (17) A backpak shouldn't hang down more than four inchs below the waist. (18) So please make sure that you are following the backpack safety rules. (19) If you do, you'll avoid back and shoulder problems later on!

Use "Check Your Backpack" to answer the questions. Write your answers in complete sentences.

1. What word is misspelled in sentence 1? Rewrite the sentence correctly.

_____

_____

2. Is more than one word misspelled in sentence 2? Use spelling rules or check a dictionary. Rewrite the sentence correctly.

_____

_____

3. Use spelling rules or check a dictionary to rewrite sentence 7 correctly.

_____

_____

4. Sometimes words are used incorrectly. Rewrite sentence 12.

_____

_____

5. What words are misspelled in sentence 17? Rewrite the sentence correctly.

_____

_____

Context Clues

Learn About It

> **Context clues** are the words and sentences around or near an unfamiliar word that help you figure out what the word means.

Read the paragraph. Use context clues to figure out the meaning of the highlighted word.

The bird's head was covered in scarlet feathers. I had never seen such a bright red color on an animal.

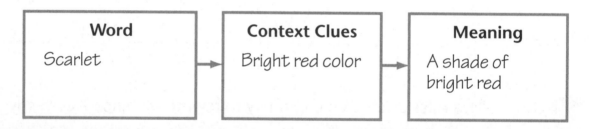

Word	Context Clues	Meaning
Scarlet	Bright red color	A shade of bright red

Context Clue Type	Meaning	Example
Synonym	A word that means the same as the unfamiliar word	The frisky cat was playful.
Antonym	A word that means the opposite of the unfamiliar word	The microscopic bug was not big enough to see.
Definition	A word's actual meaning	A telescope is a tool that makes things that are far away look closer.
Example	A list of words linked to the unfamiliar word	My mom grows tubers such as potatoes and yams.
Restatement	Saying a sentence again in a new way	The team was invincible. They could not lose.
Cause and Effect	The reason something happens and its result	Because we won the game, we were ecstatic!

Try It

Read the passage. As you read, circle unfamiliar words. Underline context clues that help you understand each word's meaning. Use the questions to help you.

Joshua Trees and Yucca Moths

Many plants spread seeds and pollen by way of bees. The Joshua tree does something else. This plant is a kind of yucca that grows in the Mojave Desert of California, Arizona, and Nevada. It depends on the yucca moth instead of the bee. Biologists, or scientists who study life forms, have come to the Mojave Desert. They want to study what happens between the moths and the Joshua trees.

Unlike bees that spread their pollen almost accidentally, the yucca moths make sure to spread pollen for the Joshua trees. The trees cannot make seeds until they get this pollen. The moths depend on the seeds from the Joshua tree to feed their caterpillars. The Joshua tree needs the moths to spread and stay alive, and the moths need the Joshua tree for food.

The scientists say that the moths use their tentacles to pick up pollen when they find a plant in bloom. Then they carry the sticky substance and deposit it on the female part of a Joshua tree flower. The moths lay their own eggs in the same part of the Joshua tree flower. Soon their larvae eat the tree's seeds. The baby caterpillars leave enough seeds for the tree to spread its seed. The Joshua tree and the yucca moth—what a team!

> **What is a *Joshua tree*? Where do you find words that tell you about it?**

> **What is a *biologist*?**

> **What are *larvae*?**

Where should you look for context clues when you find an unfamiliar word?

Apply It

Read the passage. Answer the questions on the next page.

Nervous and New

(1) Mara sat on the floor and glanced around her bedroom. (2) Everywhere she looked she saw a mess. (3) Toys were scattered here and there. (4) Shelves were half full. (5) Big cardboard boxes were half empty. (6) She felt exhausted looking around, seeing how much work she still needed to do. (7) She did like her new room. (8) The sunny yellow walls were cheerful, and light streamed through two big windows. (9) She liked the shiny, brown wooden floor, too. (10) The problem was that the new room came with a new house—and a new school. (11) Tomorrow would be her first day as the new kid, and Mara was filled with dread. (12) That feeling of fear would go away, her mom said, as soon as Mara got involved in school. (13) Mara didn't believe it for a minute. (14) She pulled a picture of her best friend out of a box and put it beside her.

(15) A sudden knock on the door startled her, and she jumped. (16) "Come in," she called.

(17) A smiling face emerged from around the edge of the door. (18) "Hi," the face said. (19) "I'm Kyra. (20) I live across the street. (21) Hey, you have some of my favorite books here! (22) You like *The Boxcar Children*, too?"

(23) Mara smiled back and felt her gloomy feelings begin to vanish. (24) How could she stay sad with this friendly neighbor around?

Use "Nervous and New" to answer the questions. Write your answers in complete sentences.

1. What does the word *glanced* mean in sentence 1?

_____

_____

2. What does the word *scattered* mean in sentence 3?

_____

_____

3. What is another word you could use for *streamed* in sentence 8?

_____

_____

4. What does the word *dread* mean in sentence 11?

_____

_____

5. What does the word *gloomy* mean in sentence 23?

_____

_____

Roots and Affixes

Learn About It

A **root** is the basic word that other parts can be added to. A root gives a word its main meaning. An **affix** is a word part that is added before or after a root. A **prefix** is an affix added at the beginning of a root word. It makes a new word with a new meaning. A **suffix** is an affix added at the end of a root word. It makes a new word with a new meaning.

Read the paragraph. Look for roots, prefixes, and suffixes.

The dance teacher moved across the room. The dance looked easy, but Julia knew it was harder than it seemed. She was thankful for the chance to preview the dance steps. The girls waiting for their turns were talking softly to each other. Julia didn't want to seem unfriendly. She just wanted to do the dance perfectly.

Word	Meaning	Root	Meaning
Teacher	One who teaches, educator	Teach	To educate
Harder	More difficult	Hard	Difficult

Prefix	Meaning	Example	Meaning
un–	Not, the opposite of	Unfriendly	Not friendly
pre–	Before	Preview	View before

Suffix	Meaning	Example	Meaning
-ly	The way something is done	Softly	Done in a quiet way
-er, -or	One who does	Dancer	One who dances
-ful	Full of	Thankful	Full of thanks

Try It

Read the passage. Underline words that have prefixes or suffixes. Use the questions to help you.

Pick a Pet

Choosing the right pet is a big decision. You should think about what you like to do for fun. Do you like nonstop action? A playful dog might be right for you. A dog needs to spend time outside running and jumping. Usually dogs are very active.

Do you dislike noise? Do you like things to be quiet and peaceful? A tank of beautiful fish might be for you. You can add plants and shells to make a lovely home for your pets. Some people find watching fish calming.

What about a cat? For the most part, cats are quieter than dogs and do not need as much space. These furry creatures like to spend some time with their owners, but they like time alone, too.

Perhaps you would like a gerbil or a hamster. These animals usually live in cages. Though they need exercise, they do not have to depend on you to help them get it. Of course, it's helpful if you buy equipment for them that will help them exercise. An exercise wheel might do the trick.

No matter what kind of pet you choose, you should be ready to take care of it. All pets need food, water, time, and kindness.

> **What root do the words *action* and *active* share?**

> **What does the word *dislike* mean? Break the word into its prefix and root.**

HOTS Understand

How does knowing an affix's meaning help you figure out the meaning of a word?

Apply It

Read the passage. Answer the questions on the next page.

A Day at the Library

(1) Mia and Abby walked into the library to work on their project. (2) Unfortunately, they did not lower their voices quickly enough. (3) "Girls, you are speaking too loudly," Mrs. Lang said sternly. (4) They both apologized to the librarian. (5) Then she smiled at them and said, "I pulled out some books and magazines that might be helpful. (6) You've got quite a weighty project."

(7) "Thank you, Mrs. Lang," both girls said. (8) They had told the librarian last Monday what they were going to be working on for their end-of-the-year project. (9) It was time to start their research.

(10) The girls moved quietly to a table and began to work. (11) They were going to write a report about animals in space. (12) They wanted to see what scientists had learned about animals and weightlessness. (13) After flipping through a book, Mia moved to a computer and began a search. (14) "Here is something about monkeys," she said. (15) "I wonder what a playful animal like a monkey thought about being in space! (16) Do you think it had to keep still?"

(17) "Oh, look!" Abby said. (18) "They sent a dog into space, too. (19) Do you think it missed its owners?" (20) The girls read on. (21) They kept working until they had enough information to make an interesting report.

Use "A Day at the Library" to answer the questions. Write your answers in complete sentences.

1. What does the word *quickly* mean in sentence 2?

_____

_____

2. What does the word *loudly* mean in sentence 3?

_____

_____

3. What does the word *helpful* mean in sentence 5?

_____

_____

4. What root do the words *weighty* and *weightlessness* share? What do the words mean?

_____

_____

5. What does the word *playful* mean in sentence 15?

_____

_____

Glossary and Dictionary

Learn About It

A **dictionary** is a book that lists words in alphabetical order. It includes definitions for each word, along with a pronunciation guide. It also lists the part of speech. If one word has multiple meanings, the dictionary will include definitions for each meaning. A **glossary** is a list of important words found at the back of some books. A glossary will include the meaning of a word as it is used in that book.

Read the glossary entry and the dictionary entry for the same word.

Glossary Entry:
design a picture showing a building's form and structure

Dictionary Entry:
de•sign (di ZINE) *verb* **1.** to make a plan for something to be built or made (*The carpenter will design a cabinet before she builds it.*) *noun* **1.** the way something is arranged (*The tile had a beautiful design.*) **2.** a sketch or plan (*The architect's design called for one bay window.*)

Glossary Entry

Gives the meaning of the word as used in the book or article in which it is found

Sometimes includes a guide on how to pronounce the word

Both

List words

Include definiton

Dictionary Entry

Gives more than one meaning of the word

Tells each word's part of speech

Shows a guide on how to pronounce the word

Shows how the word is broken into syllables

Try It

Read the passage. As you read, circle the words that have more than one meaning. Use the questions to help you.

A New Kind of Animal Shelter

(1) There have always been people who care about animals. (2) That's why people have long built shelters for stray animals. (3) In these, workers can feed and shelter cats and dogs that do not seem to have an owner. (4) People who want pets can come to the shelter and choose one. (5) Of course, people who have lost a pet can come to see if it is at the shelter.

> **What does the word *shelter* mean in the title? What does the word *shelter* mean in sentence 3?**

(6) Now architects are coming up with plans for even better animal shelters. (7) In these new buildings, both the people and the animals will enjoy a more homelike setting. (8) Planners will work with shelter owners to make sure that they are designing just what the animals need. (9) They will look at the number of animals that will be sheltered at one time. (10) They will also think about whether that number might change over the next several years. (11) They will plan an inviting space where visitors will come to meet the cats and dogs. (12) Good architects try to use plenty of natural light. (13) If the climate is warm, dog kennels might be indoor or outdoor. (14) Although it might seem as if quiet is best, often it's better for shelters to be on main roads. (15) That way, more visitors will come to adopt the animals.

> **Is *plan* used as a noun or a verb in sentence 11?**

Apply

Does the word *setting* have more than one meaning? If there were a glossary attached to this passage, what meaning would be listed?

Apply It

Read the passage. Answer the questions on the next page.

The Gullah

(1) Have you ever heard of the Gullah? (2) This group of people has a fascinating history. (3) In the 1700s, European settlers in South Carolina and Georgia figured out that the coast there was a good place to grow rice. (4) Landowners in these states found that enslaved people from West Africa were experts at growing rice. (5) Many of the enslaved were from Sierra Leone. (6) The weather there is similar to the weather in South Carolina and Georgia. (7) West Africans and their children ended up planting, growing, and harvesting rice for slave owners to market. (8) They formed a culture that mixed West African cooking, music, and crafts with American influences. (9) They became known as the Gullah.

(10) The Gullah also brought tropical diseases from Africa. (11) Slave owners would get sick if they stayed on the rice farms during the hot spring and summer months. (12) That meant the Gullah often worked on their own. (13) They did not have much contact with the outside world.

(14) After slavery ended, the Gullah stayed put. (15) They lived on the coast and on nearby islands. (16) The market for rice moved to different parts of the country. (17) Still, the Gullah kept to themselves. (18) That is why, even today, they have held on to their amazing culture.

Dictionary Entry:
mar•ket (MAR kit) *noun* **1.** a place for selling and buying food and other goods (*She went to the new market to buy apples.*) **2.** a region where goods are bought and sold (*There is a market for gold in Nevada.*) *verb* **1.** to sell goods or services (*He wanted to market his new product.*)

Use "The Gullah" to answer the questions. Use a dictionary to look up unfamiliar words. Write your answers in complete sentences.

1. What part of speech is the word *coast* in sentence 3?

_____

_____

2. What does the word *weather* mean in sentence 6? What is another meaning of the word *weather*?

_____

_____

3. Which definition of the word *market* is correct for sentence 7?

_____

_____

4. What does the word *culture* mean in sentence 8?

_____

_____

5. What does the word *contact* mean in sentence 13?

_____

_____

Literal and Nonliteral Language

Learn About It

Literal language uses the actual meaning of words. **Nonliteral language**, such as **metaphors**, **similes**, or **idioms**, are phrases or expressions used to make speech and writing more interesting. Nonliteral language does not mean exactly what it says.

Read the paragraph. Look for nonliteral language and think about what it means.

"Tess," Mom called. "You're glued to that game like gum on a shoe. It's time to turn off the computer and hit the books. Your science test is in two days. Studying is nourishment for a hungry brain."

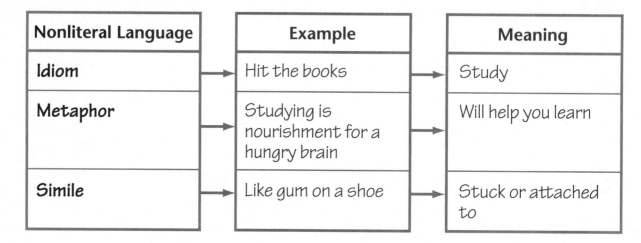

Nonliteral Language	Example	Meaning
Idiom	Hit the books	Study
Metaphor	Studying is nourishment for a hungry brain	Will help you learn
Simile	Like gum on a shoe	Stuck or attached to

Try It

Read the passage. Look at the phrases that are highlighted. Draw a box around phrases that have nonliteral meanings. Use the questions to help you.

Spring Break

Nate was sure that this vacation was going to top the rest. He was on top of the world at the idea of going to the ocean. Nate wanted to ask his best friend, Terry, to go. Nate's mom said okay, so Nate went ahead and asked him. Terry was bursting with excitement!

> Look at the first two sentences. How does Nate feel about going to the ocean?

When spring break came, Terry was packed and ready to roll. But then Nate called. Nate's mom had a van that they were planning to take to the ocean. It was as old as the hills, but it still ran. That is, until it was time to go on their trip. On the day before they were supposed to go, Nate's mom took the van in for a tune-up. She wanted it to be safe for the trip. Unfortunately, the mechanic told her that the van was a mess. He said that they could buy a used car for what it would cost to fix the van.

> What does the phrase "ready to roll" mean?

Nate was crushed and hated to tell Terry the news. Terry thought for a minute, and a lightbulb went on. "I know," said Terry. "We can ask my parents to use one of their cars."

> What does "a lightbulb went on" mean?

HOTS Analyze

Why does the author use so many nonliteral phrases?

Apply It

Read the passage. Answer the questions on the next page.

Garage Sale

"Rise and shine!" Mom shouted, trying to wake us up early on Saturday morning.

"Mom, I'm sleeping like a log," I muttered.

"Up you go," she cried. "You, too, Fred," Mom called to my brother in the next room.

Both of us just rolled over. "Just for the record, if you don't help me set up this garage sale, you don't get to share the money we make," Mom said.

That got me up. Mom left me to deal with my brother.

"Come on, Fred. We can make a killing on our old toys," I said.

Fred was not happy. Fred really likes to sleep. He started shouting about how there was no rest for the weary.

"Don't blow your top!" I said. "You'll be glad later if you get up now, especially when you see all the cold hard cash we make."

"Sharon," Fred said, "I don't think we see eye to eye on this. No one is going to spend money to buy our used toys."

"Oh, Fred," I said, "At least let's give this a try."

Finally, the two of us went to help Mom. She'd had enough of us fighting like cats and dogs. The three of us set up our things on tables. People started arriving before we were even finished setting up. "The early bird gets the worm!" one shopper said. Soon our belongings were selling like hotcakes!

Use "Garage Sale" to answer the questions. Write your answers in complete sentences.

1. What does the narrator mean when she says she is "sleeping like a log"?

_____

_____

2. What does "just for the record" mean?

_____

_____

3. What does Sharon mean when she says, "Don't blow your top"?

_____

_____

4. What does the shopper mean by saying, "The early bird gets the worm"?

_____

_____

5. What does the simile "selling like hotcakes" mean?

_____

_____

Shades of Meaning

Learn About It

> A word has two types of meanings. A word's **denotation** is a word's literal, dictionary meaning. A word's **connotation** is the mood it implies.

Read the sentences. Look for the different shades of meaning in the highlighted words.

"Listen to the bird chirping!" said Lance.
"That crow's cawing has to stop!" said Miriam.

Word	Denotation	Connotation
Chirping	Making a high-pitched sound	A pleasant, musical sound
Cawing	Making a harsh, grating sound	An annoying sound

This chart shows some examples of connotation.

Word	Denotation	Connotation	Example
Aroma	Smell, odor, scent	Enticing smell, usually coming from food	The **aroma** of the baking chicken brought me to the kitchen.
Fragrance	Smell, odor, scent	Pleasing smell, as from perfume	The perfume had a sweet **fragrance**.
Stench	Smell, odor, scent	Unpleasant and revolting smell, as in sewage	The **stench** of sulfur in the lab was overwhelming.

Try It

Read the passage. Think about words' connotations and denotations. Use the questions to help you.

Rumors

"Did you hear about the new girl who's going to be in our class?" said Jose.

"No, what?" asked Maria. She was talking to Jose on the playground outside of school.

"She's starting school next week because she just moved to the city," said Jose. "We'll have to be nice to her."

"Yeah, and I found out she's a great gymnast," said Phillip. He'd heard what they were talking about and came by to join them.

"Yeah, I heard she's won a bunch of competitions," said Jose.

"I wonder if they were local or state competitions," said Frida, who was a gymnast herself.

"Oh, I'm sure they were state," said Phillip. "Mr. Katz said he suspected she would be in national competitions before long." Mr. Katz was the librarian.

"Yes, rumor has it that her parents moved to the city just so that she could work with an expert coach here," said Jose.

"Really?" said Maria. "Hey, Johnny!" she called to one of her classmates. "Did you know about the new girl coming to our class? She's an Olympic gymnast!"

> **What is the connotation of "did you hear"?**

> **Would you be more likely to believe someone who said he or she was *sure* about something or someone who said he or she *suspected* something?**

HOTS Analyze

What effect does a word's connotation have on a reader?

Apply It

Read the passage. Answer the questions on the next page.

An Ad for Blast

Two advertising companies were competing to get work for a new sports drink called Blast. Both companies knew that they had to come up with an ad that would persuade people to buy the drink. They also knew that first they had to convince the drink company that they were the right firm to do the job.

Hans Advertising came up with a jingle that had the following words:

> *For the cheap shopper—*
> *Get a cheap, cool drink.*
> *Buy Blast Sports Drink!*
> *It's as good as you think!*

They had a woman sing the jingle on a recording. Then they got it ready for their pitch to the drink company.

Yorkshire Advertising took another approach. They put together a short film showing a mountain biker climbing up to the peak of a mountain. The biker stops at the top and takes a long drink of Blast Sports Drink. Then the viewer hears a man's voice say:

"You know what you want, and it's a Blast."

In a print advertisement, Yorkshire also highlighted the fact that Blast Sports Drink is a smart buy and that it is delicious.

When the drink company heard the two pitches, they had no trouble making up their minds. "Yorkshire wins it, hands down," said the company's president. "Why, they practically forced us to choose them."

Use "An Ad for Blast" to answer the questions. Write your answers in complete sentences.

1. In the jingle, Hans says Blast is "for the cheap shopper." Do you think people like being called *cheap*?

_____

_____

2. In their print advertisement, Yorkshire writes that Blast is a "smart buy." Does that sound more or less appealing than *cheap*?

_____

_____

3. How is *persuading* someone to buy something different than *forcing* someone?

_____

4. In the jingle, Hans writes that the drink is "as good as you think." Would that persuade you to buy it?

_____

_____

5. In their print advertisement, Yorkshire writes that Blast is "delicious." Does that make you feel more like buying it than "it's as good as you think"?

_____

_____

Academic Vocabulary

Learn About It

Academic vocabulary is made up of the words that are useful to know for particular subject areas, such as math, science, and social studies. If you do not know the meaning of a word, you can look it up in a glossary or dictionary.

Read the paragraph. Look for the academic vocabulary words.

In science, we learn about different <u>technology</u>. Human beings have used <u>tools</u> for thousands of years in order to get things done. Technology, such as <u>computers</u>, can help us learn new things and get things done.

Science	Meaning
Technology	The knowledge that scientists use to create new tools and machines
Tool	Something used to do work
Computer	A machine that processes and stores numbers, text, and pictures

Math	Meaning
Addend	One of the numbers being added in an addition problem
Difference	The answer to a subtraction problem
Factor	One of the numbers being multiplied in a multiplication problem

Social Studies	Meaning
Urban	Having to do with city life
Population	The number of people living in a certain city or region
Public transportation	System of moving people from one place to another that anyone can use (for example, city buses, subways, monorails)

Try It

Read the passage. Think about the meaning of the highlighted words. Use the questions to help you.

Learning Math

Elia thought she was ready for the big math test. She was good at addition problems, even those with big addends. She almost always could find the difference in subtraction problems, and she remembered what strategies to use. She knew her multiplication facts up through the number 5, and she could figure out the answers for higher numbers as long as she had enough time.

> How is the word *difference* as it is used in the passage different from describing the difference between two characters in a story?

So why did she panic about the test? Elia's teacher had been working hard with all of the students in the weeks before. She even had Math Camp at school on weekends. Elia went so that she could review measurements in the metric system, as well as in the United States customary system. At home, Elia's mother quizzed her on the different geometric shapes she might have to know. After a few days, Elia had no trouble telling the difference between a circle and an oval or an octagon and a hexagon.

> Where could you look to find the meaning of the word *octagon* or *hexagon*?

Even so, Elia couldn't sleep the night before the test. As she started, Elia was really worried. After sailing through a few addition problems, though, she relaxed. Elia realized that she was well prepared. She only had to use what she already knew.

 **HOTS Understand**

Why is a glossary helpful for learning academic vocabulary?

Apply It

Read the passage. Answer the questions on the next page.

Try Taking the Bus

In cities large and small, traffic can be a real problem. It sometimes seems like every living person is on the road at once. If people used public transportation instead, we could clear up the traffic. We might also clean up the air!

Some cities, like New York, have subway systems that millions of people use every day. These underground trains are fantastic, but they are very expensive to build.

Some communities have tried monorails. These are rails built on one track that runs high above the ground. Like subways, monorails can move many people without clogging up roadways. However, most urban areas have rejected monorails because people think that they also cost too much to build.

Another public transportation system is the bus. Unlike the subway or the monorail, buses are already in just about every city with a large population. Many are surprisingly comfortable. Some have two decks. These double-decker buses are great for getting a good view of your city.

If you are afraid that taking the bus will take you too long, try riding one when you are not in a hurry. Go with your family to a place where your parents usually drive. Time how long it takes to get there and back. Once you have this information, you can use it to plan your trips. Why not try taking the bus?

Use "Try Taking the Bus" to answer the questions. Write your answers in complete sentences.

1. What is *public transportation*?

_____

_____

2. What does the word *subway* mean?

_____

_____

3. What is a *monorail*?

_____

_____

4. What does the word *urban* mean?

_____

_____

5. What does the word *population* mean?

_____

_____

Graphic Organizers

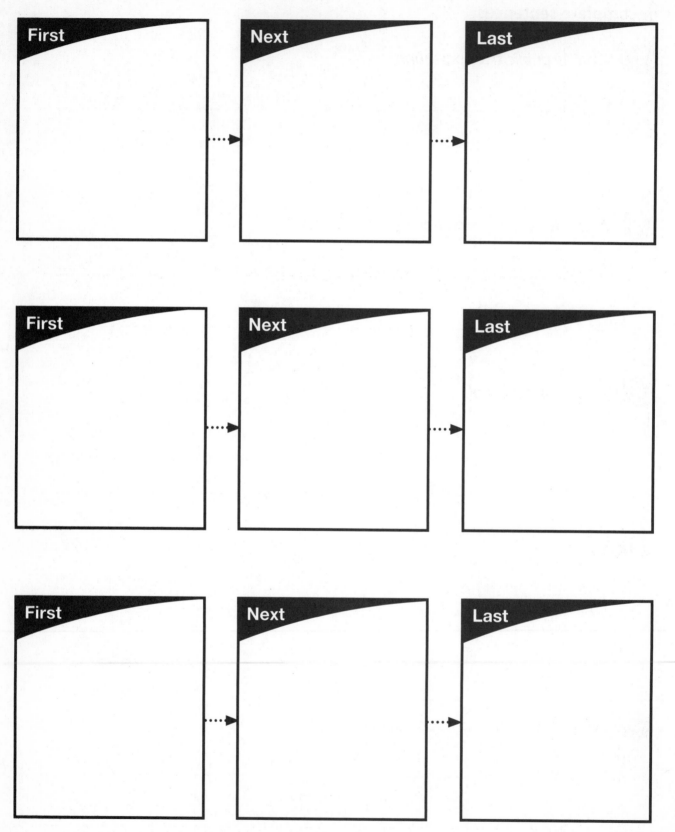

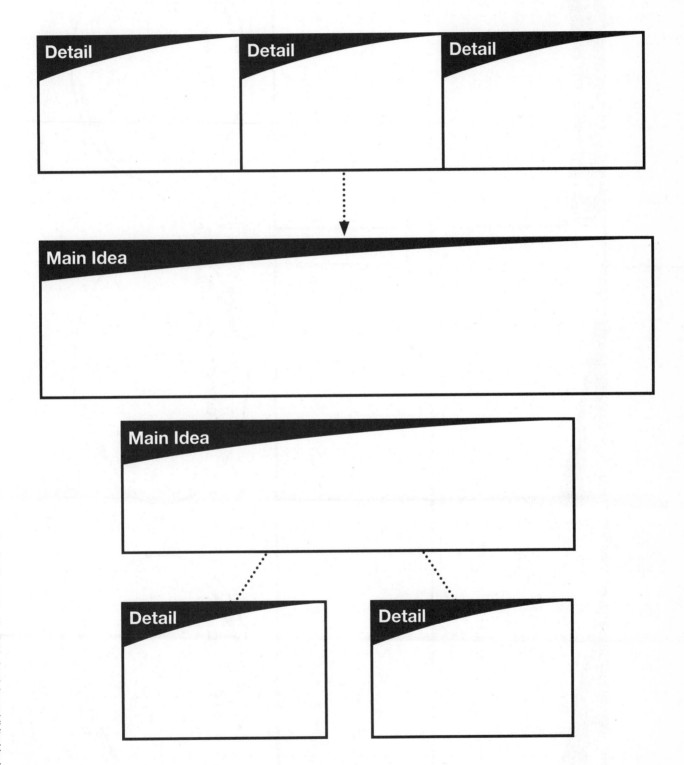

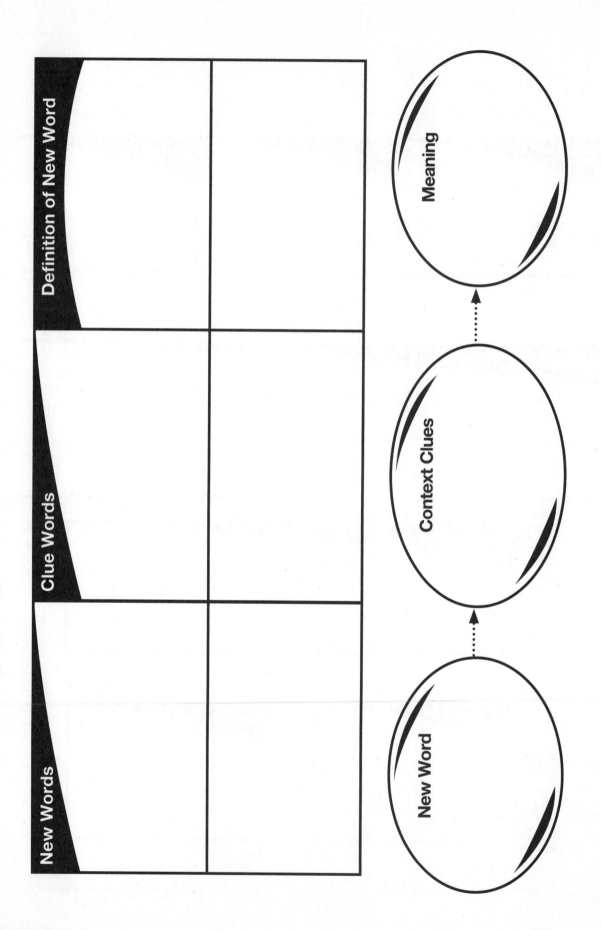

New Words	Clue Words	Definition of New Word

New Word → **Context Clues** → **Meaning**

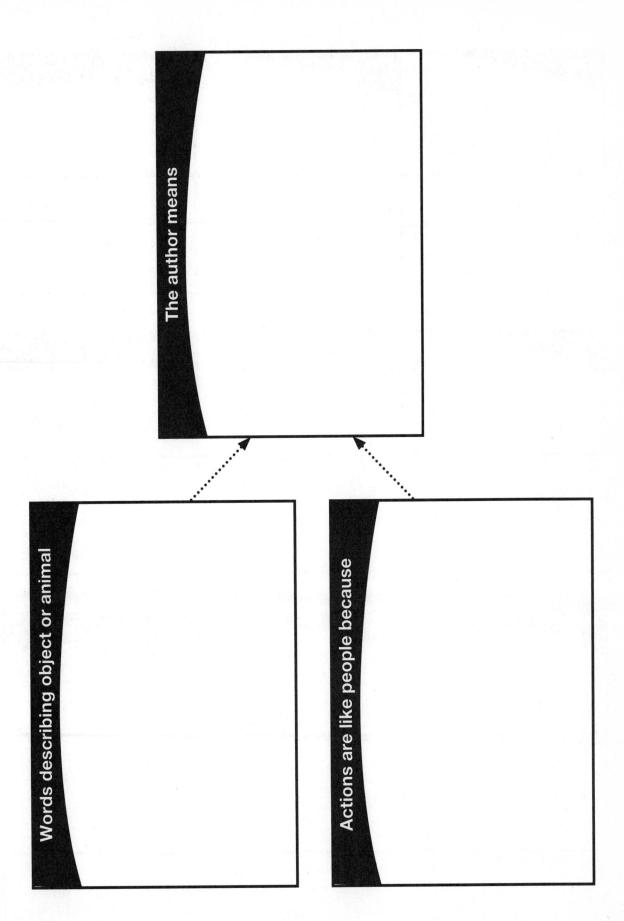

The author means

Words describing object or animal

Actions are like people because

Topic	Clues	My Conclusion

Topic	Clues	My Conclusion

Topic	Clues	My Conclusion